Love Letters

From Hades

Emily Brandt

ISBN: 9798215160619

Any references to historical events, real people, or real places are used fictitiously. Names, characters, and places are all products of the author's imagination.

Cover designed by: Alyssa Verbert

First edition printing

For more information, please email:
emilybrandt.writer@gmail.com

For Hugo. Without you, these pages would be empty.

Introduction

The story of Hades and Persephone is one that transcends the test of time. Something about it grips us in a way that much other mythology hasn't.

The dichotomy of a Goddess of Spring and the King of the Underworld captivates us. It's a theme we see repeated over and over again, even in modern literature. If you go to your local bookstore, you're bound to see one or two retellings of this myth on the shelf.

In this book, you'll spend a year with Hades. From his utter despair and loneliness in the Spring to his rebirth and rekindled love in the Winter.

I hope these pages bring you comfort and the knowledge that even the darkest of nights turn into the brightest mornings.

The Myth

Persephone was a beautiful and sweet young Goddess. Demeter, her mother, and Goddess of the Harvest, was incredibly protective of her, like mothers often are.

Hades, God of Wealth and King of the Underworld, was in search of a wife. He saw Persephone and immediately fell in love with her. After asking permission from Persephone's father, Zeus, they made a plan for Hades to kidnap Persephone and marry her.

One day, Persephone was picking narcissus flowers in a field alongside her friends. Suddenly, the world opened up, and Hades, riding in his chariot, swept Persephone off her feet and brought her down into the Underworld.

Demeter searched endlessly for her lost daughter and, in her despair, refused to care for the Earth. The world froze and plants wilted. Humanity could no longer feed itself, and the cries and pleas of humans were heard even on Olympus.

Helios, the Sun God who saw all from above, came to Demeter and told her what he had witnessed between Persephone and Hades.

Enraged, Demeter went to Zeus and demanded that Persephone be returned to her at once. Zeus obliged, and sent Hermes down to the Underworld to retrieve her.

In the Underworld, Persephone found herself alone with Hades. While she missed her mother, she was not completely unhappy and had learned to love Hades and the gardens he had planted for her.

When Hermes arrived to take Persephone with him, Hades feared that, given the choice, Persephone would not return to him. So, Hades offered her six pomegranate seeds to eat. When she ate them, Persephone was permanently bound to the Underworld. So even when she was brought back to her mother, Persephone would be forced to return to Hades.

The reuniting of Persephone and Demeter brought the world back to life. Fruits flourished, and the flowers bloomed. But it would not last forever.

For six months of the year, one for each seed, Persephone resides above with her mother. Together, they make the flowers grow and bring Spring and Summer to the world.

During the other six months, she returns to Hades to live as Queen of the Underworld. Demeter's despair returns once again, as the leaves fall and Winter arrives.

And thus, our story begins...

SPRING

My Dearest Persephone,

It feels already too long since I last felt your
embrace. I write these to you in hopes that you
remember me while we are apart.

So that you might return to me still. Even when the
world suffocates for the sake of our love.

Yours,

-H

Happiness in your

Absence

Is like smiling

At a funeral

I stand like a ghost

At the edge of our bed

Looming in the shadows

I haunt this house

When you're gone

A hollow shell of myself

Forced to fade into

Nothing

I wish my heart stayed frozen in the comfort of
Winter.

And that suffering from your hand was my task to
bear alone.

That selfish demon!

The antithesis of her gifts.

Were she not from my own kin,

I would drag her to Tartarus myself.

One such as she, who proclaims to bring life to the world,

Has taken the last living part of me.

Come back!

Come back!

Little bird

Your song once so sweet to my ears

Now only echoes

In the empty caverns of my heart

Was your cage too small?

Did I come off too strong?

Your corpse lies pale against the slate

I beg, please

Little bird, to me

Come back!

Come back!

My thoughts spiral

                    Around

                                        And

            Please,

You.   Come back   Around

                    To me.

You.   and

                    Around

        You.

Love used to be clean

Like fresh mint leaves

And empty promises

Never confused with blood-red seeds

Or wishing things to be

Black or white

Rain or snow

Love or hate

My Dearest Love,

How is it that the birds sing? Knowing that I am kept here, far below in a grave I did not make to be mine.

How is it the flowers grow? When death surrounds us all and swallows the world whole. Sucking up the lives of those who came before them.

How is it the people dance? Knowing hatred fills the air and reeks its stench through the streets. Suffocating and killing this world they claim to love.

How is it that I still surrender my heart each time? Knowing when I see you again it is only for a while, and not for life. And my heart will wilt again. Like the gardens you love so much.

Yours,

For that is all I am.

I cannot cross the veil from this world no matter how hard I claw at the film that is hung between us.

Like being set inside a frame.

Frozen, watching the world pass by before me.

High on the shelf, slamming bloodied knuckles
against the glass.

Willing it to shatter diamonds across the floor.

Even if your fingers bleed picking up the pieces,

I'll know you felt something for me.

Even after your cuts heal and the violets on your
hands disappear.

Those simple words you spoke to me still ring in
my mind.

Even now, as I lie in this dark abyss

Those words

Of youth and love

So normal, so *instinctual*

Like legs entwined beneath linen sheets

I've tattooed them on my heart so I may never
forget

I'm yours.

Remember me in the spaces between the
diamonds in the sky

and

I'll remember you in the spaces left between the
beating of my heart

I planted a garden for you in your absence

Narcissus

To remind me of that fateful day

Its yellow petals soft like sunshine

They speak of you

And your thunderstorm laugh

I stare at them and wonder

If you think of me in the darkness

And smile

You are my rain

My lips the desert

I wish to drink you in my skin

Wash away my sins

Close my eyes while I

Open my arms as you

Pour your love into me

I would give my rubies for a minute with you

Take them all

For riches are nothing

If my world is empty

Without your love

To give meaning to the suffering

If only the Spring rains would wash me clean of the memories that cling to me in gray.

Will I be enough for you?

When my hands ache?

And the tears have dried from my cheeks?

And my blood turns to water?

When my love for you is the only part of me left?

SUMMER

As the world rests,

I listen to the choir of crickets above

Singing their love cantatas to the

Moon who replies with

Silent applause

I wonder if they know how many

Find respite in their

Everlasting devotion to another who will never

Return the kindness in full

I am a Cursed man

Fated for loneliness

Pierced through the heart

With a dagger of my own design

Handle in your hand

Wrapped in mine

I keep myself locked away

In a ribbed cage

There is no lock on the door

And no one left to be saved

My body is a graveyard

Of unlived potential

And forgotten dreams

Of your eyes

And your smile

Immortality isn't fun when I spend it wishing only for death.

Orpheus came to me and wished to reverse death

A fool's errand it was

For death claims us all

Except those who long for its embrace

I tore up your portrait today

I wanted only to forget your face

So when you don't return

I can begin to clean myself

Of the memories of joy I once held

And wash away the hole

You've opened up within me

This ink, my blood, on the page as I bear my soul to
you in a way so intimate I feel only safe to shout
these words in the privacy of my mind. Were I a
braver man, I would speak the words I write, and
show you I am one worthy of your glance.

This vile, filthy life!

How cruel a world.

How cruel a wife.

To abandon one such as me.

After all we had.

All we SHARED.

My home.

       My food.

          My bed.

 I've torn all remembrance of you from

My soul.

Snipped away the traces of you from

My mind.

Never again will I be the fool of something

Such as

Love.

Sweet Honeysuckle,

Forgive me.

I know not why I said those words to you. I am a fool of my own heart. So blinded by fury and pain that I did not see. I will never be worthy of your forgiveness, but if you return to me, I will do my best to be one you can be proud of.

Loyal.

To you alone.

This is a promise I vow to you.

I await your return in silent solitude.

H

An ugly sneer and sunken face
Eyes that burn like charcoal
Spidery fingers and sharpened teeth
A foulness that follows me

The world has made me this way
Taken me from the beauty of it all
My brothers who tricked me
And forced this burden onto my shoulders

Rejected by all that is good
Eyes that do not meet mine
No lovely thing grows below
For the sun here will never touch.

But when I saw you
And your eyes met mine
You looked at me once
Then looked at me
Twice.

Remember me not as this broken man

But instead as one put back together

By the glue of your lips

And the gentle touch of your fingertips

I shall not trouble you any longer

I wish only to be a

        Faint memory...

             ...In the back of your
             mind.

Midnight Chimes

On the shortest night

I cannot sleep these days

Your silhouette haunts my thoughts

And your eyes haunt these halls

If I turn my head quick enough

I can almost see your shadow

And in the dead silence of night

I listen, even still, for your laugh

How foolish of me when I know

We still have many months to go.

The relentless waves within me drown out the

music of your voice

When you are so far away and I'm...

So...

                Far...

                        Below...

A few seeds, and your promise to me

Will you keep it in the Winter chill?

Where the only warmth in the world

Is in your smile?

I sharpen my teeth on the loneliness

that caves into me.

When will you return? For how long? Do you even
want to? Do you still love me? Do I disgust you?

Have you found another in the world you love so
much above? What can I do to be enough for you?

I dread the solstice when you leave me.

Never to return again.

The frost is coming

That frozen anger in your mother's heart

It tickles the blooms of the earth

I rejoice in the death

Knowing that soon

You'll make the journey to me

With your suitcase in hand

I'll wait open-armed

For your tender embrace

And forget the warm rains of Spring

With each shiver of the Autumn leaves

Return to me, my lark, my dove

So we may sing once again

To drown out the screams in my mind

AUTUMN

My mind beckons to shout the words I dare not say

42

(I missed you)

Loving you is in my nature

Like how the leaves fall

And petals know just when to open

It's something unspoken and unknowable

And yet I feel it all the same.

And so I find you once again

Fresh as Spring and

Sweet as the plump cherries of Summer

So alive.

Death cannot bring peace

The way you can

Oh darling,

How the world shimmers at your every glance

Do you know how it longs to kiss your feet?

And blooms at your touch?

How honey drips from your lips?

Even Narcissus forgets himself

When you come into view

Cut my heart

Let me spill onto the floor

Allow my blood to warm your hands

And find respite from the screams of Earth above

Will you ever forgive me?

For taking you away

Laying poppies at your feet

In hopes that someday

You'll see the broken man before you

And find me now complete

Once again.

I wear a mask of death
Bone white with sunken cheeks
All those who see me, fear
For I am the Reaper of Souls

Yet you came so willingly
You soften at my touch
Braiding daisies in my hair
And never saying much

Your eyes search to find me
The man behind the gate
Who quivers at your glance
And once didn't believe in fate

You dress in purple velvet
Iron makes your crown
Stone cold glare, like mine once
All who come kneel down

My heart is yours to take

I ask you to feast upon it

I will gladly let you consume all of me

For the promise of

Your forever.

I never saw the beauty in Autumn

Until you showed me the colors of the world

And suddenly I knew.

Why we must sacrifice it all.

Why the seasons must change.

And how death brings new life.

Over and over again.

Much like how I become new again

With each passing season.

I forgot my heart could beat before it saw yours

And recognized a love so pure

It finally had something to live for.

Persephone

A name like music

So sweet Apollo would not dare to play it

And those who do not think love exists

Would begin to believe

As soon as the sound of your name

Sang its melody

In their ears

You've given me all

And yet

My greedy hands

Wish to rob the graves of

Your heart

Here is the key to my house

Bring in your bags

There is no guest room

For all here is for you

Wrap yourself in my arms

My heart will keep you safe

Feast on my fruits as you wish

And stay home

Here

With me

Until you grow tired of the chains

And thorns

That wrap my heart

The tender softness of your flesh

The blooming blood that courses your veins

The gentle movements of your hair

For this

I'd give my all to you.

Of all the names I've been given:

"The Wealthy One"

"The Unseen"

"King of the Dead"

"Killer"

"Illustrious One"

My favorite one is:

Yours.

I recognize the loneliness in you.

That seeps into your skin.

Like water into the soil.

It's in me too.

A graveyard of broken hearts.

Wishing to be sewn together.

By love's red thread.

When I first saw you

The Earth began to sing

A song so honeyed

That even the Muses

Were Silenced

I wish to remember us like this

Fingers entwined like the branches of the trees

And wishing on every star

That the night never had to end.

I never cared for Aphrodite

Too vain and selfish for one such as me

I never understood her whims

While she and her son pricked humans

With those arrows so sharp even the coldest

Heart could not resist its poison

But now I understand

I see it all

Though I do not know what love is about

I finally found the meaning

And wonderment of something

Such as falling in love

My anger is a mirror

That stares me in the face

Each morning I wake up

And see the worst parts of me reflected

Do you see this part of me too?

Red

Like fury and blood

The fog that surrounds me

Until I no longer can see the world for how it is

Even when surrounded by beauty

All I can feel is pain.

Your softest touch

And heart of a lion

Reached out and tamed

The most fierce of creatures

My precious, Cerberus

Bowed to your presence

And I knew

I was Master to none

Least of all You

I pity the man who does not know the love of a
woman

    (Such as you)

Who makes men question everything about them

    (And would gladly rip their soul)

For a single glance

Imagine us in fifty years

Hands wrapped in each other's

Love still as fresh as sunrise air

Imagine us tomorrow

Two hearts beating in a rhythm

Only we can hear

Imagine us today

Crashing together like storming waves

And falling away just as fast

Only to come together again.

WINTER

Don't be afraid of the darkness, Love

Without the night

We would never see the stars

Your destructive tendencies never scared me

For the walls you break

I built just for your hands.

How funny the world works

    For one so full of life

        Chose one such as me

            Above all else

                To call yours

Fate is a funny thing

The way you are tied to me

By some invisible knot

Our hearts tied

Our souls connected until

I forget what the

Universe was like

Before you

IF a god could die

I will gladly be the first

Completely undone

By your hand

This dance we share

One, two, three

One, two, three

I never get right

My feet are too heavy

I trip on your skirt

One, two, three

One, two, three

Will I ever get it right?

The room swirls around me

I hold tight

One, two, three

One, two, three

Around and around we go...

Quiet as the dead of night

You slip into my bed

And into my arms

As Midnight sings its song

Into the shadows of the morning

The December Chill

Wakes my bones

Prickles my skin

And reddens my cheeks

(Much like falling in love)

I look at you

Amongst the frozen land

And Spring warms

The darkest parts of my heart

Do you regret it?

This barren life with me?
So different from your youth.

A withered man who claimed a heart that wasn't given.

I can manage sneers from others.

I have grown used to their cursed looks.

But from you,

I cannot bear it any longer.

I wish to see you smile again.

I tried

     I tried

          I TRIED

To love you from a distance

To keep myself away

But when I saw you there

Shattered amongst the scattered seeds

I saw in you a truth

A strength unknown to any man

One that only a woman could possess

And so

I fell

     I fell

          I FELL

And I took you down with me

For better or for worse

Together let us dance on the graves

And sing to the celestial beings

While sipping on moon juice and whispering sweet
nothings

Into a bright and golden year

The moment I saw you, I knew.

The music in your voice rang like bells in my ears.

Your eyes cut like diamonds, straight to my soul.

The beauty in your slender hands, so soft to my touch.

And when you saw me, I know you saw it too.

You've shown me time and again

How these names given to us

Are not rules to be followed.

That a maiden can become a Queen so feared that

Human hands shake.

Or a King so bold can become a simple man

Unraveled by a lover's glance.

I took a walk through your gardens

I listened to the hollow breeze that takes the
branches

And pushes the leaves up, and up

I tasted the fruit so sweet to my lips

Like Childhood

I took a walk through your gardens

And began to question fate

How lives are so entwined

Like the roots of trees

And the flowers that bloom

How the bees bring honey

So golden like the sun

And sweet like rain

I took a walk through your gardens

And saw life through your eyes

How bridges are meant to be crossed

As long as the foundation is strong

Beneath feet like stone

I took a walk through your gardens

And heard the birds sing

For the first time in ages

A melody that felt like home

And awakened the heart within

I was reminded of you

And your melancholy glare

How caged you are

At the bottom of the earth

Petal,

My dearest,

Love,

Flower,

These days you look so forlorn. If only I could raise
your spirits and kiss the wounds within your heart.

To shield you from the agony that I have caused
you.

This throbbing that never ceases amongst the
wounds in the fabric of our lives.

-H

Historians will rewrite our story. We are not
immune to the changes of time. They'll call us
many things. They'll place words on our lips that
were never spoken.

But you and I.

We will know the truths we speak in soft whispers
of the evening. When only the souls of the damned
may hear us.

I write these notes in the hope my words on the
page are clearer than the thoughts that turn to ash
on my tongue.

But how can I express my love for you when I
myself am incapable of understanding?

Please, my love, don't let my words and harsh
actions foul this love— as pure as the fountains of
Olympus.

Our love, mightier than Heracles

If I could sing, my love songs for you would
dethrone Apollo.

85

For never again would a song capture the beauty
and rarity of a love such as ours.

And never again would the poets dare to touch
their pen.

I love you like I love the Earth

For all its wonder and beauty

And

For all its ferocity and destruction

I envy Zeus no longer

For though he rules the skies

And his skin feels the warmth of the sun

He will never know the feeling

Of devotion to one

Such as I do for you

The way my heart breaks

When you turn from me

And how I count the seconds

Between each glance

Forgive me for caging you away

I forgot that a bird needs to spread its wings

In order to fly and sing

I worried a wandering eye

Might take you away in the night

Just as I did

So long ago.

I was asleep before

The souls of the Styx

Were more alive than me

Still clinging to a life

That is far forgotten now

Orpheus will play a song of our love

For centuries to come

So even when the mountains stop

Whispering your name

We will be remembered

In the melodies that fill the silence

Between the beating of lovers' hearts

I fear that you see the darkness inside of me

And that one day you will realize that

The man you love

(And who loves you so)

Was once the monster under your bed

In my mind we, two phantoms, float away from it all. High above Olympus and their *divine understanding.* Never touching the ground as our love lifts us higher and higher. Til we finally rest amongst the heavens we were kept out of for so long.

If they were to steal you away

I would make the launch of a thousand ships look
like child's play

Never would they dare cross the Lord of Death and
the Queen of the Underworld again

The days grow long again

And your mother begs you back

I wish it were not so

But our deal is iron

Will you remember my face

When the sun blinds you

And the flowers beg for your glance?

Please, my soul begs

Stay, my skin beckons

Go, my lips say

Goodbye, my love

Just for now

I'll dream of our nights together

Even when the sun wishes it never had to set

Characters

HADES- God of Wealth, King of the Underworld, husband to Persephone

PERSEPHONE- Goddess of Spring, Queen of the Underworld, wife to Hades, daughter of Demeter and Zeus

DEMETER- Goddess of the Harvest and Fertility, mother to Persephone, sister to Hades

ZEUS- God of the Sky, King of the Gods, father to Persephone, youngest brother to Hades
APOLLO- God of Music, Medicine, and Prophecy, son of Zeus

NARCISSUS- A man who was said to be so beautiful, he fell in love with his own reflection and was later turned into a flower.

ORPHEUS- A son of Apollo who traveled to Hades to ask for his wife, Eurydice, to be brought back to life. It was said his song was so beautiful it opened the gates to the Underworld and brought Hades and Persephone to tears.

THE MUSES- Nine goddesses that rule over all things art, science, and literature.

HELIOS- God of the Sun whose chariot brings the Sun across the sky.

MINTHE (MINT)- A nymph who once had Hades' favor. When she boasted that she was more beautiful than Persephone, the Queen turned her into the mint plant. It is now a sacred plant to Hades.

About the Author

Emily has been a storyteller her entire life. From the stage to the page, sharing dreams and telling tales of adventure and love are her biggest passions. *Love Letters From Hades* is her first book.